Wishy-washy Day

Story by Joy Cowley
Illustrations by Elizabeth Fuller

"It's wishy-washy day,"
said Mrs. Wishy-washy.

"Into the tub
for a scrub you go."

The cow hid in the garden.

The dog hid in the shed.

The duck hid in the closet.

The pig hid under the bed.

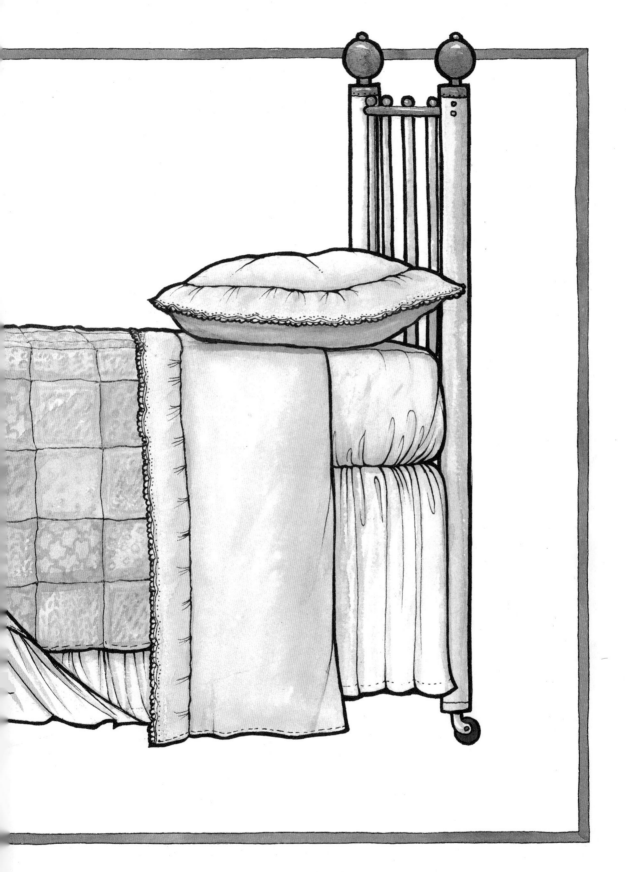

Mrs. Wishy-washy looked.

"Where have they gone?"
she said.

Then she slipped on the soap

and fell in the tub instead.

Wishy-washy! Wishy-washy!